Set sail

How to go from where you are to your destination

Louis Bassey

SET SAIL
Copyright © 2018 by Louis Bassey

Published by Impact Publishing, Ghana
Email:christianmichael02.cm@gmail.com

www.impartworld.com

+233542995931

DEDICATION

I dedicate this book to my mentor, big brother and buddy, Daniel Kelly. To whom I shall remain indebted for setting the foundation on which this book is based.

ACKNOWLEDGEMENTS

Any accomplishment requires the effort of many people and this work is not different. I thank my family especially my sister Emmanuella, whose patience and support was instrumental in accomplishing this task. My special thanks goes to the whole team behind the successful completion of this project, Christian, Coleman, Adey, Dorathy, Ferdinand, Noble and Kimberly. You guys are the best.

Grateful acknowledgement is made to; Dr. Sandy Onor, Mr. Whyte Uwem and Mr. David F. Richardson.

Most of the examples, stories and illustrations used are the result of a collection from various sources, such as; magazines, newspapers etc. Regardless of the source, I wish to express my gratitude to those who may have contributed to this work, even though anonymously.

Every effort has been made to give credit where it is due for the job well done. If inadvertently I have omitted giving credit, future publications will give due credit to those that are brought to the author's attention.

Contents

Introduction

L ife is a voyage. And we are sailors. Every soul is onward to the yonder. The good news is that we must all arrive. Though arrival is guaranteed, a destination is not assured. The difference is in the movement: whereas some make the journey, others flow in the journey.

Those that flow with the journey are they which permit life to happen to them. They wake up expecting the best from the day. But unfortunately, the best do not just happen to those who wait or those who wish but to those who make the move and GO! As wonderful as hopes and wishes are, it is never the attitude of sailors.

The attitude of sailors is one that does not support frivolity. The sailors would sing:

If you tell me, it is going to be alright, you're telling a lie

If you tell me it is going to be all smooth, I will doubt you,

If you promise to go all the way with me, I would laugh in disbelief,

I know you mean well,

But I am a sailor,

We use different vocabulary:

We call *wish*, frivolity

We read *hope*, uncertainty

And we interpret *promises*, as vain.

x

For we thus judge: if it must be done; if it must happen, we have to make it happen.

Make the move

Sailors sail, they make the move. They take the step. They take the initiative. They don't let things happen to them; life is not supposed to happen to you. **You will happen to life**. **Define a destination. Describe a direction**. **Then take the necessary action**. A continual action results in a continual progress. Nothing guarantees the destination than a continual action.

However, a continual action does not automatically shield us from oppositions. In the real sense, continual action attracts continual persecutions. But should we say that because the wind is against us, we should change our direction? Do we decide to allow the wind to choose our next direction? Those who get to their destination are clearly those who push through. **If we must be celebrated**, **at last**, **we must be willing to make the move**.

For one, **here** is good, and to another, **there** is good. But yet to some, there is a yonder to pursue. If you say I want to go *from here to there*, it sounds great. But the matter is where is there? There, may just be there. But could there be any place other than there?

Why should you stop there when you can go further?

A destination is self-defined. This makes it more difficult to determine. At the time when one is celebrating a successful arrival, a fellow sailor is beating himself for being too slow. And while soaked in a contemplative mood wondering what to do, he finds another zooms pass him to yonder.

Destination is at the yonder. Meanwhile, yonder is not a location, instead, it is a progressive location.

We have two matters at hand:

- There is a yonder for the going, AND
- There is a movement to make,

Let's pretend we didn't notice the yonder and focus on the movement. It would be more profitable to find out what manner of movement is required to journey in the right course. Of course, the seers have said, **right direction equals right destination**. The direction (movement), therefore, becomes our most revered area of concentration.

This book is dedicated to divulging the indices of movement(s) that would take us forward. As we proceed we shall be comparing the application of the operations with others who have gone ahead to yonder.

Before you proceed, answer the following questions:

- Do you agree that there is a yonder for you?
- Are you willing to make the move?

If your answers are YES! You are good to go.

Turn to the next page to proceed to collect instructions to your SET SAIL.

CHAPTER ONE

Believe

The beauty of life is in the awareness of a supreme being. That helps us to have a realization of who we actually are. The essence of life is in our personal definition of ourselves. And because we are not of ourselves, it becomes false to define ourselves by ourselves and from ourselves.

Without is a supreme being somewhere, we don't have a definition. Even those who claim that there is no God, the resultant effect of that thought is that they themselves have lost their personality. Because something in us will keep querying, 'so how did I come here; who brought us here?' If there is no source there is no purpose. If no one sent you, the truth is that you are here for nothing.

Let's look at it from this point of view: every purpose has the functionality of accountability. And it shows that if there is going to be accountability there is somebody somewhere to be accounted to. **We lie when we claim 'there is no God'**. The highest form of deception is claiming, 'there is no God'.

Our focus in the chapter is BELIEVE. And we shall be looking at it in two dimensions:

"**All things are possible to them that believe**".

1. **Believing in God**.

Believe is a simple word that helps us achieve extraordinary things. I would say that belief is at the root of every invention, every initiative, every mandate; purpose, belief is at the root of it.

Who or what you believe will determine how much you can do. Believing in God is synonymous to tapping into a superpower. It means looking beyond self and then connecting to something that is higher than you. It is the highest form of human expression of ourselves. **When we think of ourselves by ourselves and from the standpoint of ourselves**, **because we don't know ourselves very well**, **we limit ourselves**.

Now when we think of ourselves in reference to a greater power, it enables us to come out from ourselves; to attempt great things. It makes us not to worry about our ability thinking that a higher power is backing us, so we are free to express. Believing in God is beyond psyche. It is not psychology. It is, in reality, connecting to the force that makes all things go round. The greatest people on earth in the 21st century will be those people that believe in God. Believing in God is different from professing faith in a religion. It is also different from a set of rules and regulations. It is having absolute reliance and trust on the existence of a supreme being on your side. Imagine you are engaging in a project that is bigger than you. But you know about a supreme God that is on your side. And he is not just an ideology; He exists in reality and he does not need any special invitation to help you because He's already there. All you need to do is connecting to him; he gives you all the resources required.

Great things are done by great personalities. We beings are humans and we are not great. But there are things that could make us great. Connecting to a great God automatically ushers every one of us into a realm of greatness. There is no great thing that had ever happened on earth except by the backing of a higher power. Some persons chose to connect to a smaller power, like secret cults. My worry is that any other power that is not God does **'trade by barter'**. And terms and conditions are not spelled out clearly. In your mind, you would be thinking that what is presented is all. And the contract does not include **'exit'**. I could imagine that people would open their eyes and sign a contract that does not include exit without having a full understanding of what tomorrow could bring. And as soon as they get in, the truth unfolds and there is usually no log out button.

But believing in God, the terms and conditions are stated clearly from the onset. Anybody can believe in God. In the dollar Note of the United States of America, we could see this clearly shown. It is written clearly by the founding fathers, the inscription reads '*in God we trust*'. It is not a decoration. What makes a nation powerful is connecting to a powerful being. Believing in God is not a myth. It is not one of those religious jargons. It is actually an active participation in the supernatural. It is engaging the supernatural force of the universe in a natural realm for a positive realm. You are bringing down the supernatural to the natural, to make something happen in the positive. We are indirectly saying that the connecting point between the supernatural and natural is a tiny word '*belief*'.

Your achievements are simply the totality of how much you have believed in God. This book is about moving from here to there and from there to our yonder. And we know that if we depend only upon FATE, we are going to end up as another story; story that touches the heart. But if we go by FAITH;

- We have deemphasized humanity
- And we have emphasized divinity.

So our course can be predicted. The forces of the earth we don't have control over, somebody somewhere has control over them. And if we have a close relationship with the one who controls them, our journey can be predicted. When you trace the history of great inventions vis-a-vis the inventors, you will realize that all of them, let me say 90% of them have their roots traceable to GOD. Something in their genealogy runs down to God. And all of them express faith in God or there is a God. So the first thing we must do for ourselves if we must make progress is to believe in God.

Talking believing in God, some folks in certain nations do not yet believe in the existence of God. So, how do we explain this? Some persons have to believe that everything that happens is a coincidence. They live their life on default not knowing what could happen because anything can happen. So they undergo the day with fear, and they move around hoping that the best would happen. Unfortunately, most of the time, they worse usually happen.

For these folks, they only thing we can do is to help them to think. Like a story was told about a professor who believes there is no God. The young preacher tried his best to convince him but all effort proved abortive so he decided to do an experiment. For the professor, everything just came out of some coincidence of some form of chemical reactions, like the theory of a broadband explosion.

So the next morning the young preacher dropped a nice flower in front of the professor's door before he was awake to return later for the real deal. When he came back, he found the professor outside with his friends and neighbors all trying to decipher how the flower came about unfortunately for the professor, he forgot he didn't believe that things are done by people. Rather he believed that things are done by things. I think for the first time in his life, he asked the wrong question: **'who must have done this?'**So when the young preacher came in, he asked the professor what the problem was, and he explained that he found this bunch of flowers, and had since been worried to know who must have kept it.

Then the smart young man replied, 'No sir, I don't think so; it just appeared'. And they got into a small argument as the professor did his best to prove that everything continues in a state of rest unless acted upon by force. When the professors point prevailed, the young man simply added, 'this is what I mean; the earth did not just appear. Someone must have put it here'.

A wise man said, **'if there is no God**, **life will lose its essence; we would be reduced to flowers or animals'**.

Any moving object must have two reference point, where it is coming from and where it is going. If these points are not available, that object probably is not moving. In one sentence we can say that there is God. But when foolishness combines with education, it produces very funny effects.

2. Believing in self

The first thing of note is that, if indeed there is God and he created us for something great, he would have made provisions for us. He would have done some things to enable us to become our best in the sphere in which he has put us.

To believe in you is both a service to God and a service to self. Religious people would say something like 'I don't believe in myself or my belief is in God'. If indeed there's a God and He is a big God; a good God, how on earth would he give the man an assignment without providing the necessary equipment to enable them to do the work effectively.

Anybody who does not believe in himself has a foundational problem of disbelief in God. If you ask me, I would say that this disbelief is a little bit different from unbelief. Unbelief is the total absence of belief in the system. While disbelief only means that in some certain places or areas there is no belief; but generally speaking there is a form of belief available in the system. That is why in some places Jesus rebuke them for unbelief and some places for disbelief.

So what I'm saying is when we actually believe in God foundationally as a good God, we will believe in ourselves. Like that scripture in Daniel 11:32 says:

…but the people that do know their God shall be strong and do exploits.

It starts from knowing the Lord, and the result is in doing exploits on earth. There is that strength that comes from knowing the Lord.

A wise man said **God has endowed and equipped every human being to fulfill the very unique purpose for which he is created**. The first endowment is the brain. The human brain is endowed with more than 6 billion cells. This means that our human brain has the capacity to store the names and faces of the 6 billion people on earth without mistakes.

That's how powerful the box hanging on your head is.

So when we say 'we cannot' we sin against our creator. If the phone speaks and says 'I cannot make a call' the phone has reported her manufacturer. Because cell phones should make a call. So if it can't make a call it is not well produced and something is definitely amiss. Sometimes it looks like we are being humble by saying, 'I can't do it'. This is the meaning of what we are saying, 'God did not create me well, if he did, I should have been able to do this and that.

Whatever you are saying you cannot do, somebody, somewhere created by the same God is doing it. So, it could be that you were robbed; you were cheated. And God is the suspect.

Have you had young people say things like my brain cannot take such and such subjects in school? It means that God cheated them in that he gave them a lesser brain than others. And since God cheated them, it becomes even more sinful for God to demand more from them seeing that he didn't equip them. This is the same attitude portrayed by the servant in the story of the talents.

Do you remember he buried his talent inside the earth and had a thousand and one excuses why he shouldn't make an impact? The reason for his excuses is traceable to the fact that others are given five and two. So he concluded that the king is a wicked man. A wicked man is one who expects more than you are capable of delivering. And that young man in the story of the talent declared, 'you reap where you do not sow'. What his saying in essence is: 'you expect output without input'. Let me ask you, what do you say of God? Are you like that young man? Do you sometimes have a feeling that God's requirements from us are far beyond our abilities? And this made him a wicked God?

If you're still following, you'll understand that we are saying that believing in yourself is a physical demonstration that you believe in God. I can now say that no one believes himself without first believing in God. The issue of low self-esteem is a matter of lack of faith in God. We must have pulled our eyes away from God before we confidently declare we are nothing. We are something because somebody made us something and called us something. You know that scripture which says 'we are wonderfully and fearfully made; marvelous are your works'. It is beyond our comprehension.

I would like us to agree that we are capable. Here's a quote by Marianne Deborah Williamson and it reads:

> *"Our deepest fear is not that we are inadequate. Our deepest fear is that we are powerful beyond measure. It is our light, not our darkness that most frightens us".*

A wise man once said, 'if you can think it, you can achieve it'. This means for any thought to have passed through the paths of our mind, it's an indication that shows there had been a pre-installed ability to execute it within. As far as you can think it, you can do it.

First prerequisite to move to your yonder (success) is telling yourself, 'I am the right person on the pitch right now; I am the best trained; best equipped, color, location, best breed to do what you are designed to do. This does not mean that no other person can do it. But no one can do it like you. You're best fitted for that task.

Not believing in yourself is a disservice to yourself and to humanity. Believing in yourself uncorks the reality on the inside. Learn to separate fact from the truth. Let your attitude be this:

Whatever I'm doing now, including the negative things, does not truly define me. I am on the inside. I'm yet to be revealed. I'm a mystery. I'm evolving I'm coming out it's just a matter of time.

This is the meaning of hope; this is faith. I may be down now, but it does not change the truth that I'm powerful. I'm an explorer of the gold mine called me. The machine is just too powerful, just that I'm going through the manual.

My matter is only a special case of ignorance. There's no issue with ability and capability at all. Not a problem of lack of ability. I'm able. It's just that we're going through the manual; the machine is huge and very dynamic. You have to tap the world on the back and say, 'world wait for me I'm coming'. Let me just go through very fast. I'm coming. I'll soon step on the stage to the backend and the whole light will be on me.

Now, it doesn't matter what my family is saying. And it doesn't matter what my background is saying. I'm coming. There is a time of the arising. Even for a man named, John the Baptist, it was said that he was hidden till the time of his appearing.

The action point is to explore. Embark on discovering you. It has nothing to do with sex, race or color. The black folks keep complaining, 'it's because I'm black'. I thought it was a matter with the black until I heard the white complain, 'because I'm white…' Then I realized that it was not a geographical matter. Our matter is more psychological than geographical.

'There is greatness within you'. Les Brown

Take a moment and close your eyes and imagine the biggest you can. If you have done so, here this:

If you can conceive it, believe it, you can achieve it. Zig Ziglar

When you believe in yourself by believing in God, you combine divinity and humanity. And that means that anything could happen.

"If you can?" Said Jesus, **"everything is possible for him who believes"**. **Mark 9:23**

One day, a man looked at the moon, and said, can't we go up there and check it out? Some persons argued but later it was a reality. The other time some guys observed the birds maybe and wondered, 'why can't we fly birds from one place to another'. It was argued again. Time passed and one day the Wright brothers did it. First, it looked impossible that an iron would float on the water. Today heavy ships are floating on water. Nothing is impossible to them that believe.

When you truly believe in yourself, you don't spend time looking for excuses. But you will soon find out a way. Those who do great things are those who would dare imagine more.

Though imagination is free, most persons fear to imagine.

Imagination + believe = greatness.

If you do not believe in yourself, you disable your abilities. Unbelief is a special case of disability. Currently, not having limbs; arms is no longer a disability. There are several folks who are doing great things without arms, legs and eyes. Have you heard of the great composer, Fanny Crosby who was blind from early age or Pastor Vick Vujicic, born without limbs but making global impact today? Disability has been redefined; it is unbelief. What functions of your body has been disabled via unbelief?

The truth is that God has made every one of us complete for the task. To uncover your potentials you must believe in yourself. Some persons have wonderful excuses why they are not moving forward. Excuses like 'no one believes in me. Before you proceed, let me inform you:

How possibly can you believe in what you do not know? It was even difficult for humanity to believe in God until Jesus came. Either you like it or not, seeing is believing. Show us what you got and we would believe in you.

One thing about external belief system is that it does avail nothing. Even if I believe in you but you do not believe in yourself, you'll make no progress. The opposite is also true, even if I chose not to believe in you but you took enough courage to believe in yourself, you'll make it happen. Now putting it together, 'what benefit is there in sorting for people to believe in us as a prerequisite to make progress?'

Set Sail

Therefore, instead of sitting down there praying, crying, wishing that some good man somewhere will show up and believe in you; a friend, a neighbor, a pastor, an Imam or just any person, take your three steps backward to the place of thought and believe in yourself. For if you believe in yourself, that'll make all the difference.

CHAPTER TWO

Know What You Stand For: Purpose

We are not all the same. We do not have the same destination. Though our journey be the same, our destination, and direction be not the same. One goes North through path A, another goes West through Path A while some go East via Path C, not forgetting those who go South through Path D. There are several issues concerning the journey to our yonder.

The Issue of Destination

It is no longer news that **a wrong direction leads definitely to a wrong destination**. The first thing to ascertain before we make our journey is, our destination. What do you call destination? Purpose is where we are going; purpose is both where we are going and also how we are going there. When destination is not defined, direction cannot be correct.

Only a fool takes a journey before verifying the destination. Destination determines direction, and not the other way round. We plot our journey, not from where we are, but from where we are going. When the end point is clear, the path can be sorted out.

Definition of Destination

Purpose is where we are going. The creator had wired every one of us to accomplish a given assignment on earth. Purpose is our definition. It is the original intent why we were sent here on earth. It is the problem we are called to solve. When purpose is defined, motivation is inevitable.

Purpose is our uniqueness. It is the very difference between us and others. Your purpose is the core of you. It is in you. It is the only thing that resonates within you. **Success is nothing**, **outside the place of purpose**.

Purpose Defines Success

We do not succeed unless we are becoming; we are advancing steadily towards our yonder. Every one of us suffers the danger of pseudo-success. Pseudo-success is a situation; it is a phenomenon; it is succeeding in the wrong thing. It is taking a wrong path towards a right destination. It is arriving at someone else's yonder. You have a unique yonder.

And because our soul is connected to it, nothing else satisfies like it. We may not know it at the moment, but we'll definitely know when we do not arrive there. Nothing else fulfills like when we are fulfilling something. And the man is wired to derive fulfillment in a course he perceives that is higher than him; a mandate that transcends the natural realm.

We all are inclined to doing something worthwhile, even if it means dying for it. **There is that chord within our soul**, **every one of us if struck makes melody**. Every one of us make music; we make music all the time. Some are pleasant to the ears while others are not. But there is a music that is within us that has not been sung. And it may never be sung. It may never be heard. That is your music. That is your destiny.

The world waits for that dimension. We all want to hear and feel that song. It takes several people quite some years to identify it. And because it is buried within us, we must make the search; we must search within; it is a matter of discovery.

The Issue of Diversion

We pursue hard to find every other thing but us. We take it so lightly. We allow complacency to overtake us at this junction where reality is decided. Nothing is as real as you. Nothing is as interesting as you. You can't be any better. You have to be used. Who are you?

The toughest question to ask: it'd demand your all. Yes! It is hard work to find you. Could this be the reason for the drifting? Could this be the reason for the compromise? We compromise when we do not go our way. We compromise when we do not live our dreams. We compromise, when we do not live according to our purpose; when we do not follow our path.

Beneath the struggle to be us, is the fear of being different. We wrestle with the thought, '**why should I go this direction**, **when everyone is heading this direction**'. What we didn't realize is that everyone wrestled with this same question and failed. We only joined the bandwagon of losers; those who cannot decide for themselves. And we are only applying ourselves wrongly and painfully enough, we know it.

The next question of study would be:

> *'Why should you follow them, when you can go your own way?'*

Finding your path

Some persons would be asking, how do I find my path? That's usually the wrong question. The path is not to be found but discovered. If you want to find something, you have to embark on a search. The attitude of seekers is to go out; to launch forth. And on the other hand, the miner focus on going in; launching deep.

You won't be launching out; you will be launching deep. You would be digging deep. You are not outside. You are not in the seminar hall; you are not on the field. You are not out there. You are in here. Yes! You are within. So I will counsel you, 'look within!'

Look within

When you look forward, you'll see obstacles. When you look behind you see regrets. When you look around you see people. But when you look within, you find YOU. And *You* is what you need. You need You to believe in You. You is the mystery to be known. You is the custodian of a unique dimension.

We don't listen. Even when we ask the most important question, 'who am I?' we do not wait enough to get the answer. We get distracted, with much asking, and little listening. If only you had listened to the impulses within.

There is this pull; there is this prompting. It may not be obvious but it is evident. If we allow ourselves, killing all the logic that has been keeping us from setting sail; if we let our intuition lead, we would confess that our ship is drifting towards a direction. It may be an unpopular direction though, but we keep going. Even while some of us are headed Tarshish, from time to time, our mind keeps turning towards Nineveh.

If you can answer these questions correctly and sincerely:

- Where are you going physically and where are you going mentally?
- Where would you have gone if you could go anywhere?
- What would you have done if you could do anything at all, without any constraint?

What is it that makes you live. It could be coming to you like an idea, a feeling or a prompting. You could be one decision away from the life you desired to live.

Purpose and Passion

You don't have a problem of lack of passion. You are suffering from disconnection. You are suffering from deceleration. It could be that the way you are headed, you are not wired to go that way. The unfortunate situation is that whereas we are going east, our body faculties are going west. When this situation occurs, real progress is hampered.

Decide to make the move

You may do this.

You can go your own way.

You can defile the popular opinion

You can upturn the norm.

You can make a mark.

You can impress yourself.

It starts with a decision to be You.

CHAPTER THREE

Be You

No man becomes anything great in life by being someone else; fake doesn't last long. Relevance in our world today is in being you. It is of no use becoming someone else, everybody has been taken and you can't function as excellently as the owner of the personality you took. It's therefore, wisdom that you accept yourself. *Be you for no one can be the real you apart from you.*

To be yourself in a world that is constantly trying to make you something else is the greatest

accomplishment"   −Ralph   Waldo Emerson

Limitation begins when a man starts imitating another person's Structure. In a world as ours, being you looks like a mission impossible. Every single individual has a unique expectation for you. Your friend would want you to be a talkative, on the contrary, your husband demands that you talk scarcely. Your pastor wants you to be a gentle, calm, sister/brother, as against your neighbors that say you are the caretaker so you have to be loud, not soft.

Following the wishes, thoughts, advice, ideas, and expectations of everyone around you would only give You a dangerous disease called, "comparison". Because you want everybody's applause, you end up comparing yourself with someone else. You force yourself to do what Mr. A, B, C &D says at almost same time even though you are not supposed to. You project someone else in your stead in whatever you are doing, you say things like, "I wish I can be her", "if I do this thing like this Peter may just not be my friend anymore", "if only I could walk like him" etc. Meanwhile, the truth is that if you are exactly the way that girl or that boy is, then your usefulness in the world is terminated.

The disease, comparison is the bedrock for irrelevance. If you want to gain irrelevance you just go ahead comparing yourself every now and then with someone else and puff! The deed is done. Comparison, like fixing your eyes everywhere, makes you less focused thereby achieving little or nothing.

I know the story of a young girl who was always wanting to be someone else. She would always compare herself with someone else, in her words, "my eyes are too small, I wish they were as big as Joy's, my hair is not so beautiful, if only it could be as dark as Emily's, my height is not perfect, God would have made me as exactly as Ella, if only I could smile like Pat or sing like Zoe, if only I had Lizzy's walking step or Angela's. She'd go on and on saying these things to herself until she hated her whole being and decides to begin dressing, talking, walking differently. It continued like that for months until she lost herself completely.

Now, this lady had a very alluring voice even though she didn't like it, she had lost it in her efforts to be someone else. A time came years later when there was a need for her kind of voice in one of the biggest voice over companies in the world. This has been her dream all through the time she was growing up so, of course, she applied for the job.

During the interview, she was asked to listen to an audio and try mimicking the voice she would hear. Guess whose voice was played in the audio, yes, you guessed right. It was hers, the audio was one of the practice she did whilst she was in need of a job some time ago. Seeing that she didn't get the job, she felt the voice could be the problem, so she began practicing to talk in another person's voice and that was the end of her relevance. She lost the job that day and went back in tears.

Unfortunately, this is someone's plight today. It is disheartening to discover that people no longer appreciate who they are, they prefer being someone else. The pressure from all round is also a variable to comparison. Are you losing yourself already? Is the pressure from peers, family members, well-wishing men and women, neighbors and colleagues already pulling you out of your real self? You have got to fight it, don't let that happen. If you do, you have lost your relevance. Ingris Begman says, **be yourself**, **the world worships the original**. Nobody loves fake, not even you. So, take the bull by the horn and BE YOURSELF.

A wise man said:

> *"From the time we are small, we learn to compare ourselves to others. At a young age, it is our way of making sense of things, of figuring out our place in the world. This can be fine if you have a strong sense of self and self-esteem."*

The Only cure for the disease called comparison is a Strong sense of self and/or good self-esteem. This word, self-esteem has been said to mean a lot of things by a lot of people. Before I talk on what self-esteem is, I would say what it is not.

Self-esteem is not being bossy, "feeling yourself" always pushing people around to do your bidding. That's pride!

Self-esteem is not being the first to always Speak, That could be showing off!

It is not being around everywhere doing everything, that's busybody!

Self-esteem is not pride nor showing off neither is it, busybody, it's knowing who you are. It comes as a result of understanding the person you are meant to be. It is the value you give yourself, how you carry yourself because of the understanding you have about who you are.

There are several kinds of self-esteem, they are high and low self-esteem. When you know who you are, you'd treat others well. Bosses who do not treat their employees well are only having issues with low self-esteem.

CHAPTER FOUR

Get knowledge

It is no longer news that we are in a knowledge-driven age. The difference between individuals have largely shifted. As we move from one generation to another, it keeps being adjusted. Now is the gap narrower than ever. The several variables that were reckoned with have all been narrowed to one super word, **knowledge**.

While knowledge involves the acquisition of information; wisdom is the application of knowledge. So invariably we need both knowledge and wisdom to proceed in our set sail. We are not all the same. We are not all on the same plain. The container 'age' can no longer hold us. Even the corner, 'class' can't keep us together. In fact, the variable class has been greatly redefined. It is no longer what we used to know. There is this great drifting happening in different industries, men migrating and finding their Niche. The niche is the word used to refer to what separates us. At the root of it all is knowledge.

They may be colleagues from the same school but when the real meets reality, each will soon find their niche. Knowledge is a strong force. It pulls; it rearranges a group faster than any machine could do. Gather a group from different fields at random and keep them for a while. After some time, those who are meant for the top will regroup and find themselves there, while those who are meant for the bottom will also rearrange and meet themselves over there.

The question in your mind may not be far from what I have been asking, 'how do we determine those who are meant for the top'. The answer is simpler than you would think: 'we do not need to determine anything; something within them separates them'.

Knowledge is the difference between the poor guy on the street and the rich boss in the glass house; between the successful business guru on top of the system and the grumbling entrepreneur behind the tattered kiosk. Knowledge is both power and might. It demystifies the riddle of success and places every one of us on the same pedestal. Knowledge makes it easier for us all to have equal opportunity to attempt and achieve great things.

This is the hard truth: **you are where you are because of what you know**, **and you are one**

knowledge away from where you wish to be.

On this premise, we can conclude *that we are the architects of our tomorrow and the designers of our yonder.* If indeed knowledge affects our experience, it would equally mean that our satisfaction with our current knowledge level is the killer disease we need to tackle. We shall quickly add that the flexibility of knowledge would not tolerate the inflexibility in some men.

Thus the best counsel whatsoever for the man on the journey to yonder would be, **Get Knowledge**. Meanwhile, we must know that getting knowledge alone won't do the job, but getting relevant knowledge. Though knowledge must be pursued, to maximize its produce, it must be engaged strategically. We must note that not all who get knowledge finally make it to their yonder; those whose knives are pointed strike deeper.

There are three categories of knowledge every man who made any progress had:

- Knowledge of Current location
- Knowledge of the desired position
- Knowledge of the process

Knowledge of Current location

It takes just more than advice for a man to settle down to logically consider his current location. We are all consumed with where we are headed that we forget where we stand at the moment. Some persons have even declared that knowing where they are has nothing to contribute to their destiny, thus can be ignored. They make us believe they can make a move without any reference to their point of origin, a theory that does not have any bearing in mechanics.

If it is a motion, there must be two points of reference:

- **Where you are coming from** (**current location**)
- **Where you are going** (**intended location or ideal**).

Where these variables are not resolved, we cannot say that movement is taking place. It could be either that body is vibrating or rotating. **'To vibrate is not the same as to be vibrant'**. *Christian Michael.*

Like me, you may be wondering why it is difficult to want to consider where we currently stand. I will show you:

> *There is no task so exhausting*
>
> *No activity so humbling*
>
> *And no action so demanding as knowing where we stand on the current.*

So we rather hide under the umbrella of hope than to engage in it. We know when we do, we have a lot at stake. If for nothing, we may lose our swollen ego. But unfortunately, **he that does not know where he stands**, **is a brother to him that does not know where he is headed**. Progress starts at the point when we make the decision to find our current location. We cannot accurately find our True North unless we are willing to know the truth.

While some persons are actually ready to shake themselves free from the dreamland. Some are poor but do not know because they do not understand: so they act and look rich. The only deliverance they need is someone who will wake them up.

Knowledge of the desired position

Have you imagined flying a plane without a compass? Have you imagined plying a ship without a map? **Why attempt to make the move when you are not sure of where you are headed**? He that does not know what he seeks, how shall he identify it when he finds it?

Success is not a location; success is rather a position. We can comfortably describe it as a progressive location. However, **we must know that success has a definition**. When you hit success, you won't mistake it for failure. When you touchstone, you won't mistake it for wood.

One thing about knowing where you are headed is that it instills this required sense of urgency and sustains motivation. Nothing keeps a man stagnant as comfort; nothing keeps a man restless and enthusiastic as the joy of a beautiful tomorrow.

The future you cannot picture, **you cannot feature**. **Bishop D**. **Oyedepo**

There is no better way to do this than sitting down and designing where you are headed. Write is as clearly as possible. The scriptures recommended:

Write the vision, **make it plain upon tables**, **so that he that sees may that read it**. **Hab**. 2:2

Many times, when we read this scripture, we begin to imagine that we are writing the vision for others to run with. But when we check closely, you will understand that it doesn't matter who reads it. The thing is, you can read it, and anyone, can run. This includes you.

Those who are currently running with their vision to their yonder, **are those who have read it**.

The rest of the people are either crawling or walking. The difference is in the knowing of where you are going. Knowledge of destination affects the speed of acceleration. A wise man once said, if you don't know where you are going, everywhere will appear like a junction. Perhaps I should ask you today, 'where are you going? You must be able to answer this question in a second, if not, something has to happen, and it must be now.

Knowledge of the process

Some of us need some kind of briefing so that we can settle down and journey. Before the aircraft takes off, the attendant is mandated to do a compulsory briefing to all the passengers onboard the flight. This is to enable everyone *on the know*. And as the flight commences, the pilot keeps updating the passengers on all the progress made so far in the journey. The briefing handles every internal agitation. So that passengers can focus on the destination while enjoying the journey. Now imagine boarding a flight without this necessary knowledge of the process of the journey. The tension will be too high.

You need to have a fair knowledge of the process. To move from point A to point B requires a lot. In-between this two points, a lot will happen. You need to find out what to expect and how to respond to it.

When this is resolved, the journey becomes smoother. From this point forward, we shall be looking at the process and how to respond.

CHAPTER FIVE

Develop a conviction

The winds will blow in due time, and every conviction will be tested. Conviction is not the resolve to go somewhere. It is rather a state that erupts after a resolve; an internal conclusion to become something, to go a direction, to do a thing or two. Conviction does not always make sense.

The first problem that confronts every conviction is that we all want it to make some sense at least. We want someone, anyone to endorse it; to say A YES or give a nod in approval. Then when we don't get any, we begin to falter. **We forget that conviction is a personal belonging**. **Conviction gives us definition**.

Your conviction is personal

There are two issues here. Firstly, no one is mandated to understand your conviction. Pride makes us feel like everyone should and must believe in what we believe. At one point or the other, we all have fallen into the temptation of attempting to impose our conviction on others. My conviction, your conviction, is personal.

This means that no one must believe in it. It also means that, even if no one agrees to go all the way with you, it does not and primarily should not diminish your conviction. This is actually what makes your conviction personal. Let us quickly review the indices of a conviction.

Indices of a conviction

By indices, I mean the intrinsic components that makeup conviction. When we say, conviction, and these things are not found, we lie. What are they?

1. Vision

Men go as far as they can see. Men pursue what they could see. No one can run unless he reads what has been written. It is only injustice to require a man to run who has not seen the writings on the tablets.

What affects your behavior and ultimately your direction is what you can see or what you saw. There is this fire on the mountain that only you can see. Most times we try to explain it, but we find out that no vocabulary is sufficient to articulate it. **Every one of us who has followed a vision must have met with the old man**, **'misunderstanding'**.

They can't believe because you couldn't communicate it. And you can't communicate it because it is beyond vocabulary. You see, it is personal.

2. **Decision**

Decision can be defined as the resolve to follow a course. It does not happen from the outside. It takes place within the center of a man's soul, along the corridors of will and emotion. No one can touch your decision. Again, a million persons may be around you, talking and laughing with you while you are battling and making a decision.

No one can influence your decision. People could make suggestions, and that's all they can do. But you choose whose suggestion you will let in and permit to take root. Even at the moment, you select their suggestion, they would not be aware. This makes decision a very private asset or private liability as the case may be.

3. Determination

Determination is the will to move in line with your decision and the willingness to keep going against all odds.

Several persons are made to believe that we generate determination at the point of action, perhaps as an emergency response formula to hardship. This is a fallacy. This error accounts for why many fail flat in the face of adversity.

Determination, genuine determination happens in an environment of zero crisis. It is a pre-response module against life's ups and downs. We adjust our will with such a resolution that tends to beat oncoming whatever. When we straighten our mind, and toughen our emotion thus, **'even if the worse happens**, **I will keep moving'**. This is determination.

Now when this happens no one will be present. It doesn't matter how close they are to you at the moment, the resolve happens on the inside. That makes it personal.

We could then say:

> **Vision + decision + determination = CONVICTION**

We can excuse every human if they do not understand our conviction because they are not supposed to; they cannot understand it.

Conviction gives us identity

Men are defined according to their resolve. Our internal resolve shapes us. It is the propeller that moves us or rather drives us.

What you are now, what you will be tomorrow are all tied to your conviction. You cannot rise above your conviction. You can only grow to meet your conviction. **Your conviction is the speedometer of your destiny**.

To change your result, you have to change your pursuit; and to change your pursuit you have to change your conviction. Therefore, to change your result, you need to change your conviction. A change in conviction equals a change in direction, and a change in direction equals a change in destination.

High rising men are men of high convictions.

> **'A man of wrong conviction is preferable to a man of no conviction'**
> *Christian Michael.*

My question now is, do we call that man a man who does not have a conviction. Without conviction, men don't live they exist. To exist means to drift; to suspend on the waters and allow the wave to carry us on. No sailor would try that. This is because the waves no matter how mild do not understand your destination. And because everything is moving has a destination, the wave also has a destination. It's just that you might not like it.

Men of renown; men of valor; trailblazers all have one thing in common, **Conviction**. Conviction is the hidden code of great achievers. When you pick them from different nations, religion, faith, gender, you will find this in them. Either it is in the tyrannous rule of Adolph Hitler or the peaceful but forceful negotiation formula by Mahatma Gandhi, you will find.

Conviction is a non-negotiable requirement if you must go from where you are currently to your yonder. It is a disposition that won't accept 'giving up' as an option. It is an attitude that won't allow the barking of the dogs in the valley to deter it from taking the flight to destiny.

Conviction is a decision. Conviction is a function of maturity. Take a moment and answer the following questions:

Do you really know what you want out of life?

Are you ready to pursue until you get?

Would you dance the music of ignorant people?

Do you have a conviction?

CHAPTER SIX

Practice Discipline

Discipline is about the most fearful word in the equation of success. Several persons would do everything within their capacity to avoid it. This D word is probably the most misunderstood word in history. When you hear or read Discipline, what comes to mind?

For some persons, dangerous images of some tough and very demanding taskmaster forcing us to do what on earth and in heaven we could not do. We conjure up pictures of an oppressor taking it out on his victims or a military commander drilling his boys.

This distortion in definition has made it impossible for several persons to attain certain heights of success. They do everything but discipline. Some men would joke, 'opposite of enjoyment is discipline'. So they indirectly view those who discipline themselves as suffering. Now here is the problem: attempting to succeed without discipline is like attempting to swim without allowing water to touch your head.

A certain fellow went to learn how to swim but would not allow his head to be submerged inside the water. His instructor tried all he could, but nothing happened. The fellow was breaking fundamentally a major principle of swimming. Discipline is a fundamental principle of success; discipline is fundamental.

There is no known shortcut around it. If you must succeed, you must be disciplined. If you want to succeed more, you need to be more disciplined. The rate of success you are enjoying now is directly proportional to the amount of discipline you have. **If you raise the bar within**, **you affect the outcome without**. To some persons, this might be a bad news to them. They had worked very hard to avoid any life of discipline, hoping to themselves that they could escape it. And now, someone is positioning discipline as the gate to successful living. For these kinds of people, what you need is definition orientation.

What Discipline is Not

Every one of us has a misconception of the word discipline most of which we carried from high school. Some have it in one degree and others in another. But we understand that a mistake in definition equals a mistake in operation. When the definition is not clear, advancement will be counterproductive. Therefore, we shall start by taking an overview of what discipline is by first reviewing what it is not.

1. **Discipline is a set of rules and regulations**.

Sets of rules and regulations that govern behavior and conduct in a given place are better seen as law or standard. This has nothing to do with discipline. One can have all kinds of laws, principles, and standards but still, lack discipline. And lack of discipline could result in a slack in impact.

Those who consider discipline to be impact, bound themselves with several rules. You'll find rules like, 'I don't eat this; I don't go there…' If you ask a weight expert, you would understand that laws don't operate themselves. It takes discipline to operate principles.

2. **Discipline is a life of boredom**

The poor define life as a place of luxury while the rich define life as a place of work. And because our definition of life varies, our definition of fun would differ. If you take a sample opinion on what fun is and what fun is not, you would be amazed at what you'd find. One point every one of us would agree on is that there is nothing funny in being a failure.

Discipline doesn't remove fun out of life. In fact, those who had disciplined themselves enjoy life the most. The student who had disciplined herself to study before the exam, relax and enjoy more during the exam. Adults who discipline themselves to save during their active years spend their retirement in fulfillment.

3. Discipline is penitence

Self-inflicted sorrow is not discipline. Punishment is not discipline. Discipline is rather the opposite of these two. When we do discipline ourselves, we escape sorrow and punishment. Sorrow or punishment is a repercussion of not living a life of discipline. It is an attempt to impose discipline on a life that has refused to practice discipline. Does it work?

Before you answer, just remember that people go to jail and spend ten years and come out to become worse. There were not disciplined after all. This is because discipline is internal; it is personal; it works on the mind. And no one can set our mind other than us, no matter how they try.

4. Discipline is not exertion on self

For several persons, discipline is a special form of self-exertion. When you come to them with the concept of discipline, they immediately begin to imagine how they would exact such energy on their 'rebellious self'.

The idea is that our body is such a stubborn stuff. It cannot really go our direction unless we have to push it; unless we add extra energy and revise it to where we want it to go. If not, like a he-goat, it would run off-tangent. And ultimately self-discipline is a way to achieve.

For these folks, self-discipline exists because our body is stubborn. What if what we think of our body is wrong? What if we do not know how the body functions? What if we discover that the body is our slave? What then would be the correct definition of discipline?

What discipline really is...

First, discipline is an act of will. Discipline is first an adjustment of will, then an act of will. This is foremost and ideal; an enticement; an attraction.

This attraction luring the heart away creates a distraction by causing an internal commotion. This **disturbance** (commotion) makes it difficult if not impossible for the mind-shift to regain its previous or original state. Therefore, any other attempt away from this direction causes or raises a negative signal called, **guilt** via a communication channel known as **conscience**.

The heart has caught a picture of a promised land. The body is ready to go all the way. **Discipline, therefore, is the movement strategy to go there (yonder).** Though the body is ready and her faculties are willing, movement is not guaranteed. There is the need for that harmony. There is the need for a strategy. This is because, '**for every destination, there is a predetermined**

strategy'. And when the strategy is not defined, tragedy is inevitable.

Discipline is a strategy. It is the game plan to go yonder. Not everyone has this plan. They wish, pray, cry, and even try to go yonder. But without a game plan, there cannot be a movement. *Getting a game plan and sticking to it, is the act of discipline.*

Discipline in relation to success

When you are ready to set sail, you must ask yourself these two questions:

- Where am I going?
- And how do I get there? (this is what I call strategy)

Discipline is the way forward. Those who go the way are not just those who have the *will* to go the way, but those who are ready to follow through.

Set Sail

What you are unwilling to do, regarding your yonder, several persons are already doing it. The result you have, cannot be farther than how far you are willing to go. There are those who talk, sing and dance about the journey but won't move a foot toward it.

If you want more, be more —Jim Rohn

As for you, you are not among those who talk the talk; you are a doer; you are a mover; you are a shaker. You are not among those who wait for things to happen. You are among the very few that makes things happen.

Life has not left us without a guild. We are not left without a trail. In whatever direction destiny is calling, there are trails.

If Michael Jordan had not come, someone would still be thinking that Basketball is an impossible feat. If Tiger Woods did not come, someone would still be thinking that Golf is impossible. If Christiano Ronaldo and Lionel Messi did not come, someone would still be thinking that soccer is impossible. Wherever you turn, in whatever industry or profession, there had more than once existed a champion whose trail is still evident in the sand of time.

The smartest question would have been how they did it. How did they defy the laws of mediocrity?

It was noted:

Tiger Woods used to have 13-hour marathon training days when he was younger, according to his former trainer, Hank Haney.

Do you still want to go yonder? You know better now. Let's proceed to look at the process.

CHAPTER SEVEN

Love the process

It's true that you want to move from here to there and to yonder. It is also true that you can make that move. Do good things happen to people all of a sudden?

This is the worry of several persons. They wonder why it takes some persons just few energy and short time (for so they thought), to make it through. And they imagine that it is taking more time than necessary for them to break through. And the next is usually the monsters called, discontentment, discouragement, and depression.

When we omit the process in the equation of success, we set ourselves up for frustration. This is not peculiar to anyone. It is the just one of those rules that only successful people know. Life teaches us that the process component cannot be omitted.

The plumber knows that just tapping into the water body beneath is not all there is to do. He must endeavor to move it from there to yonder. And that talks about the process.

The farmer understands that the day you sow is not necessarily the day you reap. If you must reap you must not only sow but must also be willing to wait till the day of harvest.

The student knows that gaining admission into the university is not the same as graduating from the university. You must focus on the process if you must come out on the other side of victory.

That distance between matriculation and convocation is the process.

Even if you want to fly, you have to take off and it is different from when you eventually land. There are different principles and operations involved in each.

The pregnant woman understands that being pregnant today cannot bring forth a child tomorrow. She has to wait for 9 months with all kinds of psychological and physiological torture. However, she has an understanding that the day of celebration must definitely come. But she has to pay attention to the process; she must love the process.

If she does not love the process:

You could abort the process

If she doesn't love the process, she could abort it. She could get tired and 'flush' everything out.

Like the story was told about a young man who went to cut down a huge tree. After exacting much effort in the process, he decided to retire. He, not realizing how far he has gone, turned back and walked away. And the tree was only a few meters away from falling. This is because he did not love the process.

She could refuse to be committed to the process.

The distance between where we are and where we are going is **the Process**. If we must get to that position, we must pay attention to the process. Commitment to the process is the only guarantee to the destination. But if we do not love the process, we would not commit to it.

Commitment to the process means engaging in those rules that keep the baby inside healthy and kicking, preparing for the arrival. Some ladies who do not understand this end up having deformed babies or stillbirth experience. Complete delivery must be by giving detailed attention to the process.

She could be struggling with the process

Struggling with the process leads to murmuring, complaining and self-hatred. When we struggle with the process, we cheat ourselves. Remaining in a process we are not happy about, is self-hatred. Dissatisfaction stinks; it makes us stink. We lose potential partners and run out of favor with others who would have been instrumental in bringing to pass the intention within.

The Issue of Focus

Our focus affects our perspective, and our perspective affects our feelings, and our feelings determine the outcome. Majorly, our problem is a matter of focus. Where is your focus? Where do you think a pregnant woman's focus would be during the conception period? Her focus, which typifies the focus of successful people is two:

1. Focus on what you are becoming

She is moving from one phase to another. After this process, her status would be changed forever. She would become a mother and it cannot be reversed. Do you know that it doesn't matter if the baby comes through or not? She had experienced pregnancy.

No one can call her barren. She could tell one or two lessons to a first-time pregnant woman. She has grown in the process. **When we thus focus on what we are becoming in the process**, **we'll settle down knowing that there is no loss**, **whatsoever**.

2. Focus on the destination

The bible talked about Jesus, '**for the joy that was set before him**, **he endured the cross [process], despising the shame'**. **Heb.12:2** (emphasis added).

From this scripture, we know that something led to all those perseverance. Of course, the Lord Jesus is a role model to several persons. And we would be very smart to emulate. In fact, the scripture says:

> **Looking unto Jesus** the author and finisher of our faith; who for the joy that was set before him endured the cross, despising the shame, and is set down at the right hand of the throne of God. Heb. 12:2 KJV

Great men are great because of what they know that we don't know. In the real sense, it is about what they know that we have refused to know.

Set Sail

Several persons talk about secrets to success, but are the principles of success really secret?

Like what we learned from our Lord Jesus. He endured the cross and came out a champion, this is the secret: He focused on the destination rather than the challenges of the journey. What could replace the cry of a new life to a pregnant woman? There is nothing like unto it. Just in seconds, the tears, the fears, and the sorrows are all gone and never to be remembered. The smiles of victory; the celebration; the jubilation of friends and neighbors; the sweet words from husband; nothing like unto it.

After that victory tour, whatever it is that is the pain, is absolutely negligible. She would move it; she would go the way. Even it means having to cry through. It doesn't matter how you would do it but go through it.

Love the process. Trust the process. If you would only persevere. You would only continue. Sometimes you may have momentary doubts. You may experience momentary setbacks. It could be some form of disappointment. But we know, if you could go through, you would come through; if you would endure, you would be celebrated.

CHAPTER EIGHT

Be Patient

Character is a platform for genuine growth. It is the right application of God's word. The strength of a man is his character. A nation that loses her character loses great wealth. The maturity of a man is dependent on his character strength. Charisma cannot be substituted for character. Character is what sustains a man at the top. The trace of any downfall is as a result of character bankruptcy. A wise man said, '**if you lose wealth you lose nothing; if you lose health you lose something**. **If you lose character**, **you lose everything'**.

It, therefore, explains that the hope of glory is character. It is also imperative to note that we cannot go further than who we are. *The you in you determine who you become.* It determines your altitude on earth. Men who took this aspect of their life for granted never fail to face the consequences. Having established this fact, we shall know what makes for character.

Patience a character

> **And not only that**, **but also we glory in tribulation**, **knowing that tribulations produce perseverance and perseverance**, **character**, **and character**, **hope**. Rom. 5:3-4

Patience is character. Patience is a result of several experiences, trails, and afflictions; it is a product of experiences. Tribulation gives patience its capacity to mature. A typical illustration is the story of Joseph. How did he become the governor of Egypt?

Everybody want to scale the utmost; many want to get to the top to sail. Very few care to know *the how*. No man jumps into success, there is always the how. Growth is indispensable. We grow into whatever thing we want to become. Joseph acceptance of his dream gave him opportunities to be tried: sold by his brothers, became a slave in Potiphar's house, tempted by his master's wife but refused the offer.

Patience is a brave attitude. It is the attitude that reveals every hidden aspect of man. The challenges of Joseph was programmed to make him mature. Most people receive free offers of romantic pleasures and called it love, grace or favor. **To set sail**, **you need a bearing that will serve as a coordinate**, **which is patience**.

Patience is the waiting capacity. Patience is maturity. Challenges lead to perseverance;

complaining drains the energy to sail. A patient man or woman is one who can bear up under any form of pressure without complaining.

To set sail in a life of destiny, one must develop the capacity to endure difficult times. Like the saying goes; tough times don't last, but tough people do. We are one decision away from reality: I must get to my destination, no matter what. Having the destination in mind, one can bear up under any storm that appears to blow one away from destiny. **Sticking to the end is patience**.

Many persons see patience as a waste of time. *'Better is the end of a thing than the beginning thereof'*, King Solomon. The points that give space to regrets, discouragement, and quitting is lack of patience. **Patience is the winning attitude**. Patience gets the gold out of the earth. It takes patience to bring forth.

To persevere is not to get on but to keep on. It is a call to press on; to get at it. It stresses the saying, 'it is not over until it is over'. If you would continue even when others would stop, you are outstanding.

Several persons can start a thing. The problem is not about starting. Starters do not win; finishers do. To win, we must understand this very principle, patience.

Misconceptions of patience

Patience as a word receives a lot of interpretation among several folks. And some which are misinterpretations. Lets review a few:

Patience as suffering

For some persons, when they hear *'be patient'*, the picture they get is that of a suffering old man who has no hope of tomorrow. They interpret patience as an exercise into frivolity. Something you cannot trust. They do not put the process into consideration. For them, there is nothing to look forward to. So they have concluded that 'be patient' is a polite way of saying 'take heart'.

Patience as obstruction

There are those who view Patience as an unnecessary stoppage on the path of destiny. They do not believe that stopping is part of the journey and as such, patience is totally out of the picture. They try as much as possible and as hard as possible to avoid anything that would cause delay.

Thus the receive patience as obstruction; something to avoid; something that can be avoided and more importantly should be avoided. And they consider a man who is waiting through the process as a man who has been obstructed.

Patience as failure

The worse of all are those who consider patience as failure. They are aggressive; they are scared. They are willing to do anything to avoid the waiting time. They tell themselves, if I'm found waiting, everyone would think that I have failed. So they try as much as possible not to wait.

This is the problem with a lot of fellows. When they encounter any delay, they grin in so much anger that you may want to begin to wonder, what exactly is the matter with this guy?

The effect of the misconception of patience

When your conception about patience is not proper, you will have the following tendencies:

Hasten the process

Cutting corners is synonymous with impatient folks. They won't follow the main route to anywhere. They won't obey they traffic light of life. They want it fast, and they want it here and now (instant gratification).

But yet there is a process. They won't just give way. They are subjected to go through the process. So they reason within themselves, 'how do I shorten this process?' If a pregnant woman asks this question, what do you think would be her next line of action? Induction[1].

Lack of attention to details

Impatient people do not care much for details. They are only interested in the end result. They are not concerned with the *how* to, the result is none of their business. I believe they have forgotten that **'the end justifies the means'**.

_____

[1]Induction is a medical term used refer to the process of forcing a baby to come out from the womb before it naturally comes out.

They hurriedly achieved the result but forget that the little cracks they left on the wall can cause a total collapse of the building.

Future, **damaged**

Two men went to build. One hurriedly arranged his house upon the sand and zoomed off to receive the award of the fastest builder. Meanwhile the other fellow was busy digging the soil in other to plant his house deep into the earth. Though he finished late, both of them finished eventually. Then something happened: just about when they award party would begin, it started raining.

The house of the first guy, not been properly founded on the earth collapsed helplessly. As the ceremony unfolds, hopes were high, and observers were excited. Then it was time for the men to show their work. The first hurriedly went to reveal what a magnificent building he had dropped. But to his amazement, it was gone. Meanwhile, the rain helped to wash clean the house of the second guy, revealing its dazzling beauty.

Benefit of patience

On a closer look, patience is rewarding. We may not be able to quantify it, but for the sake of studies, we have streamlined to three:

Impatience is suicidal

Some folks do not understand wait. They only know, 'move'. They do not naturally stop unless something forces them to stop. You understand what it means for something to force you to stop when you are on speed.

Most persons were not just stopped but their destinies were stopped as well. Can you imagine a car that only moves and cannot stop; a car without the brake system? The best place for the car to operate would be in heaven. But on earth here, I doubt.

Patience saves cost

The cost of building once and for all is definitely better than the cost of building and having to rebuild. *If it is worth doing, do it with all thy might.*

Patience means durability

Durables take time. The best elements on the earth crust take more time to mine. The more the time to mine, the more priced the element. Nothing good comes easily; nothing enduring comes quickly. Waiting does not only define you, but it also distinguishes you. Good things are still happening to those who refuse to give up. You are next in line if you do not give up.

CHAPTER NINE

Develop an attitude of gratitude

Gratitude is a humbling act. It is the easiest way to demonstrate humility. Everyone is proud by default. We learn to be modest and humble. Someone, will always think, 'I deserve more; I need more; I want more; I can get more...' We focus on these thoughts until we totally forget to be grateful for the little things we have received.

What we forgot ultimately is that big things are the combination of several small things. It is the little things that are added together that gives you something big. A wise man said, '**what we**

do not appreciate, **we depreciate'**. And 'to not be grateful is to be a great fool'.

Why must we be grateful?

1. **We often have more than acknowledged**.

It's good to aspire for the top; for the best. However, when we aspire for the best with little attention to the rest, we expire. Life is not only about the getting; life is more than accumulations.

Our attitudes may not defer much from that of Oliver twist who always wants more. More, and more we keep chasing until we forget what we already have. And what we forget, we have lost. When we take time to count our eggs, we invariably appreciate their individual uniqueness. Most times, the only thing you need to align back properly is to sit back and look back at how far you have come.

Though we are not where we need to be, **we are not where we used to be**.
Joyce Meyer

Though when we look ahead we can't see our destination, also when we look behind, we can't find the shore. It shows that we have made progress. And we can be grateful for that.

2. **We are far better than others**

We have been warned by our parents severally not to compare ourselves with others. And we have been taught the danger of comparison. These things we have held religiously for years. But today, we shall bend that rule a little bit.

We want to be truly grateful. Since gratitude happens from the mind, we would want to get ourselves in positions where we can engage our logic to find sufficient reason to be grateful. At first, we looked behind and we found out how far we have gone, now we shall look around, to see how well we are doing.

It's normal to be so engrossed in the journey that you have not found time lately to look around. Of course, it is not proper to be looking around very often. Take just a moment, consider other folks who are journeying with you. Have they all made it? Most likely not. If you check very closely, you likely find one or two, who are counting your current position as a high goal to attain. That alone is a reason to be grateful.

3. **All we have we have received**

Jesus told a story about a rich man who was later referred to as a fool.

Here is the story:

And he spake a parable unto them, saying, the ground of a certain rich man brought forth plentifully:

And he thought within himself, saying, what shall I do because I have no room where to bestow my fruits?

And he said, this will I do: I will pull down my barns, and build greater, and there will I bestow all my fruits and my goods.

And I will say to my soul, <u>Soul, thou hast much goods laid up for many years; take thine ease, eat, drink, and be merry</u>.

But God said unto him, <u>Thou fool</u>, this night thy soul shall be required of thee: then whose shall those things be, which thou hast provided?

Luke 12:16–20

Acquiring wealth is not the problem. Being wealthy is never an issue. But being ungrateful makes us fools. A fool counts his blessings and concludes that he had acquired by his strength alone. Pride tells us that we did it by ourselves so if we must be grateful, it must be to ourselves. How true is this?

According to John Maxwell, *one is too small a number to achieve great things*'. Whatever the feat is you didn't do it alone. First, there is an invisible force behind all our successes. When we think of where our breath came from, we'd understand that we owe someone somewhere an appreciation. Then we start to think of all who have contributed in one way or the other, both tangible and intangible. Putting all these together, to be grateful is not just a choice, it is a requirement.

Gratitude does these 3 things for us

Gratitude has been found to be a success strategy. There are things just maintaining a grateful heart should achieve. Let's look at this three I consider major.

1. Gratitude brings favor

Wherever you find a grateful heart, you will undoubtedly find honor. And honor is the doorway to favor.

Gratitude is an aura that attracts people around. Everyone wants to help or assist a grateful person. This is because gratitude is one attribute every one admires despite the age, sex, or race enjoy. Gratitude cut across nationality. First, we receive and show that we are grateful, then we keep the door open forever.

2. Gratitude relieves us of stress

Life is full of stress but stress is not a disease. It is a body reaction that can be well managed by adjusting our body disposition. And because stress is fundamentally a matter of the mind, a shift in mindset could be only what we need to get ahead.

The lesser the stress the higher the focus and the greater the impact. So whatever handles our stress, is a plus in our pursuit to a life of success. And gratitude does this work perfectly. Let's look at it.

Stress is caused by wrong focus; when we start looking at the negative side of things, we tend to worry and become anxious. Gratitude, on the other hand, adjusts our focus on the positive side of life. Whenever we say things like, 'Thank God I'm alive', it displaces every thought of death looming around us. Then you can imagine what would happen when we begin to consciously thank God for every single area of our life that we have made just a little progress. A heavy shift will occur in our productivity because we would have displaced all negativity that is slowing us down and replaced them with life.

3. **Creates an atmosphere of creativity**

Creativity is possible in an atmosphere of Joy. The way murmuring and complaining creates an atmosphere of death and shuts down the mind, gratitude trigger and enables creativity. The excited team always wins. Several persons play but the team that's grateful that they are playing in the first place and considers it an opportunity to do her best usually beats the rest. **Gratitude is a winning attitude**.

Gratitude is cultivated

Character does not come to us naturally. Nothing good does. We must make an effort to get what we want. The good news is that all we want is within our reach, but we must make the move to get them. We must also decide to what extent we want them. This is the matter.

We may be admiring a certain attribute but without a commensurate action, nothing positive would happen. The million dollar question now is:

How do we cultivate an attitude of gratitude?

The keyword here is cultivate. This implies that we would be looking at some set of principles.

Be decisive

Every great step starts with a decision. Decision is the seed of action. You must first decide to be a grateful person, just the way we all decide to be filled with complaints. We can decide to fill ourselves with some life by deciding to be grateful.

Be intentional

If you wait for what you should be grateful to pop up, then you'd wait forever. Look around to find it. Now you have decided to be grateful, search out what you need to be grateful about. When you see it, take your time and verbalize it. Tell someone about it. Talk only grateful talks, and insist yourself to always be grateful.

Be committed

'Consistency is maturity', *Christian Michael.* Now that you have started, don't stop. Keep keeping on until it becomes a part of you.

CHAPTER TEN

Love Work and Work

Work does not kill, lack of work does. It is not enough to want to succeed. It is not enough to pray to succeed. If two men want to succeed, but one chooses to sit down and start praying while the other goes out to work, it's most likely that the one who went out to work will succeed faster.

Work is not first about what we do or not. Work is first about our attitude towards success. It is the revelation of our disposition to moving from here to there and then to yonder. Why do some people succeed and other people fail? A lot of experts have proffered several solutions to this. But something is found prominent, *work*.

The attitude of work

One best-kept secret of the rich is an attitude that loves work. The poor folks have a misconstrued definition of work. The poor define work as suffering. If you interact with the poor, you could sense the feeling meters away. There is this feeling that wishes work does not exist. There is this understanding that there is a realm where work will no longer be required. And most envy the rich, as those who do not work. Or somehow, even if they do work, it must be lesser than the poor.

Perhaps you have already echoed, 'Yes!' That would be too fast for you to do. Let's review the work attitude of some successful people:

Donald Trump

Donald Trump is currently the president of the United States of America. And he is the richest president of the United States ever, as a billionaire in dollars. He asserts that '**you don't get to be a celebrity**, **business magnate**, **real estate tycoon**, **and presidential candidate without sacrificing some rest**'.

It is on record that Trump attributes credits to his success, to the fact that he gets three to four hours of sleep each night. In his words, 'how does someone that's sleeping 12 and 14 hours a day compete with someone that's sleeping three or four?'

Thomas Edison

Edison considers sleep a royal waste of time. He was one of the most famous inventors that ever existed. Among other things, he invented the light bulb. Like Trump, Edison got three or four hours sleep daily. It was reported that Edison once worked 72 hours without rest or breaks.

Martha Stewart

This great woman doesn't need any introduction. She has achieved quite a great amount and she didn't do it on her bed. She was reported to also maintain a routine of three to four hours sleep each night.

We are not trying to communicate that lack of sleep automatically means high productivity. We also understand these men have learned how to choose their battlefields wisely and maintain a consistent rest and leisure schedule. But one thing is sure, greatness does not come on the bed. Greatness does not happen to people in the dream. There has never been an award for the best sleepers of the century.

How we handle our night, reflects how we handle our finances. How we handle our bed shows in our bank account. Sleep is good for our health, but too much sleep is not good for our finances. Money is usually buried in the field. If you zoom out, you may not find it. It may require some digging.

> **'Poor is he who works with a negligent and idle hand, but the hand of the diligent makes *him* rich.' Prov. 10:4(Amplified)**

From this scripture, one can say that it is just a matter of time. To the lazy, poverty is inevitable. The same is true concerning hard work. Hard work does not return void. A young man asked a successful old man, what his secret of success. The old man replied, **'the secret to my success are three: *work, work, and work.*'**

If you don't like work, you don't like money. If you don't like work, you end up working for those who like it. The truth is, everyone must work. But liking work tends to be a better strategy than avoiding it. When we love what we do, we tend to find ways to do it better and easier.

Success without work is a scam. If it is genuine, there must be the work factor in it. Don't tolerate your mind desiring riches without work. It is an attitude that tends to poverty. Work is the tradition of the successful.

Work, the tradition of the successful

A wise man said opportunity usually dress in the garment of work. So whereas the poor are busy looking for an opportunity while avoiding work, the rich are looking for work, thus meeting opportunities.

Begging is the only work that has been mastered by the poor. It doesn't seem to cost them anything to beg. Now the opposite is true: begging is the only work the rich dread to do.

They could do anything but not begging. In fact, the fear of begging someday, somewhere, drives them to keep working. For the rich, it is either making it or nothing.

He may be riding a limousine today but that does not mean he started off with a limo, except for very few exceptions. Every one of the rich guys I have studied pride themselves with the fact that there are not afraid to lose what they've got because if peradventure they do, they'll go right back and get them all. This is huge for me because it makes me ask, 'where will they poor be at that time when a man who has been brought down by nature will stand and climb back up? Could it be that there is something these guys know that we don't?

Work is the answer. For the rich, no work is demeaning. It's only a phase. You can be down here today, and tomorrow, you go right up there, if you are consistent enough.

Work and leisure

> **Thus the heavens and the earth were finished**, **and all the host of them**.
>
> **And on the seventh day**, **God ended his work which he had made; and he rested on the seventh day from all his work which he had made**. Gen 2:1–2

Don't get this twisted. There must be rest. If you work, work, with little rest, you experience a reduction in productivity in work. And at a point, you would be in the danger of experiencing burn out. And burn out, is an enemy to creativity.

Even the rich folks we mentioned above, all of them know how to integrate work with leisure. As well as a work schedule, there is also rest schedule. A work schedule without a rest schedule is absolutely counterproductive. If I am asked to review the productivity potential of anyone, I would not ask for their work schedule but their rest schedule.

We are most likely prone to obeying our rest schedule than our work schedule. And **the ability to manage your rest schedule is productivity**. We want to take a moment to look at God's rest schedule:

In summary: **God worked six days and rested on the seventh day**.

Work six days and rest one day

The problem is that we want to work for one day and rest for six days. This is actually where the problem starts from. When we exalt rest above work, we cause confusion in the system.

Fraud is anything that seeks to exalt rest above work; treating work as an abomination. They would speak you into believing that work is as a result of poverty, whereas poverty is as a result of lack of work.

Unfortunately, no poor person wants to admit that they're lazy. They react almost usually violently whenever you want to confront their laziness. The code of poverty is usually, 'there is nothing I can do'. Really? Okay! Let's assume that there is really nothing you can do about the situation; the government and the system is not favorable to you. And it's not easy finding a job. That's fine.

Then I asked one gentleman the same question in a different way: 'so what are you doing now?' He went as thus, **'just resting and doing one or two stuffs for myself'**. And this is the problem; always resting. What if *rest* was not in the picture; what if you are not resting, what would you have been doing? I know for some people, the answer would still be resting, because they have programmed their mind to look for reasons to find some rest. And as surely you want to seek for, you will find.

When I probed further, 'why didn't you do the work?' His reply was, 'I don't have a laptop computer'. 'What about your roommate?' I enquired. This answer might shock you:

> *He came back very late with his laptop, and before then I have slept, and he woke up very early and went to work with it before I ever work up'.*

Did you notice anything? This young man was at home resting throughout the day, then slept before the one who went to work arrived and could not wake up till his partner went to work. So we have a case of sleeping early and rising late, then sleeping throughout the day. Now let me ask you, why should this guy not be poor? Why should he not be broke?

Instead of looking for a reason or a way to work, he is busy looking for excuses not to and finding some reasons to back it up. The way of the poor is the way of excuses. They are experts in excuses. And all these gears towards resting.

> **Whereas rest is good, we must not substitute our best for a rest.**

Work like a pro

> **If the iron be blunt, and he does not whet the edge, then must he put to more strength: but wisdom is profitable to direct. Eccl 10:10**

Hard work leads to success. This does not in any way imply that we must do it hard to succeed. Success is embedded in hard work. It is inside the hard work; that we would succeed. Few people understand that difficult tasks all have simple approaches that would get them done. But I think the Pros know about this.

> *Anyone can do it slow and steady but the Pro does it fast and efficient*—Christian Michael

Suffering is not impact. Suffering is not diligence. To be slow is not to be efficient. To be poor is not to be committed. If you do it once, and you are paid, then you can triple your speed to be more paid. Some people are averse to speed. They have all kinds of explanation that support slow, where slow means suffering.

Wisdom is the ability to find out how to do it easier and better. It is working smart. 'Wisdom is profitable to direct'. Whatever the job is, there could be a better and smarter way to do it and still achieve the same desired result.

You are rated for the result, not for the process. One secretary could insist on editing 200 page project word for word, as a means of maintaining efficiency. While another secretary could employ the use of some software to handle the content editing and do just proofreading to handle the context. The same would achieve the same result but at a different pace.

Effectiveness is achieving the result following the due process; efficiency is doing the same work in less time and with little resources.

Efficiency has gained another name in the business world, **working smart**, a term which did not exist until men started engaging their brain for productivity. We must work, but we can work smarter. It is normal for people who are using their brain to use those who are not using theirs. Like every other thing of life, working smart is optional.

A wise man said, 'I prefer to sharpen my cutlass for 6 months and work for 6 days than to sharpen my cutlass for 6 days and work 6 months'. This is the summary of the concept of working smart.

Working unto impact.

Know why you are working. Vision is the key. It doesn't matter where you started off if you know where you are going, then, it's fine. Right now, you may be working for someone, and you don't have much savings in your bank account if you know where you are going, then, it's okay.

We have stories like: a certain time I was working for so and so, but now, he is working for me. The beginning may be small, but the end will show those who are focused; those who had plans; who knew why they were working.

Personal development

In your workings, work on yourself. If you work in a job, you'll earn money. If you work on a project, you'll make progress. If you work for someone else, you can be sacked. If you work for yourself, you can run at a loss. But if you work on yourself, you'll make a fortune.

If you have any work that is preventing you from working on yourself, it is time to quit. Everything has a short lifespan compared to you. If you have just one place to invest, make it yourself. Consider investing in yourself a capital investment.

Don't let any day pass without you investing in yourself. One way to be sure that your tomorrow is guaranteed is that you are constantly becoming the kind of man that can suit your tomorrow. Work is always the answer.

For any observation or further enquiry, Louis Bassey can be reached directly with the contact details;

Email – Louisorok@gmail.com

Phone – +2347034873310

Printed in Great Britain
by Amazon